Colour in the words and draw a picture below to ma

THE NORMANS IN BRITAIN

The tiny mouse is hiding on every page of this book also. See if you can find him again! Write his name on the line below.

My mouse is called _____

2 William takes control

 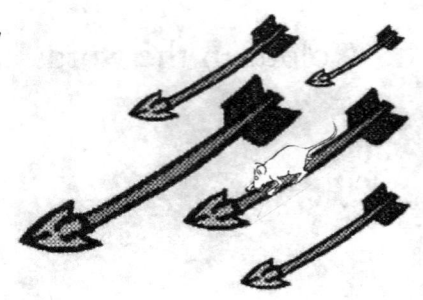

Read 'The Middle Ages' page 17 and answer the questions below in full sentences.

1. When did William win the Battle of Hastings?

_____

_____

2. What did William do after winning the battle?

_____

_____

3. What made people think William would be hard on his enemies?

_____

_____

4. Where and when was William crowned King of England?

_____

_____

5. Why do you think William was called 'The Conqueror'?

_____

_____

KEY WORD

Using a ruler underline the correct meaning of the key word below:

conqueror

- a person who does not like violence.
- a person who wins by using force.

William's Problems

William the Conqueror had many problems after he won the English crown. Study the sources below and answer the questions which follow.

William's problems

> King Harold's men do not like me because I defeated and killed their king. Some of these men are still in London.

> The Danes would still like to take over England. People tell me that they are plotting with the English in the north of the country.

> There are English soldiers in the south of the country also, in a castle at Dover. They might attack my army.

What were the three main problems William faced after the Battle of Hastings?

A _____

_____

_____

_____

B _____

_____

_____

_____

C _____

_____

_____

_____

4 William's solutions

Source 1

'Then William marched to Dover which was held by a large army. The English were afraid and prepared to surrender, but our men set fire to the castle and most of it was destroyed.'

Written by William of Poitiers about 1071.

Source 2

'William laid waste Sussex, Kent, Hampshire and Surrey, and slaughtered many people who lived there. He was then met by Londoners who gave in to him.'

Florence of Worcester, describing what William was doing before he went to London. Florence was a man!

Source 3

'The King's army approached York only to find out that the Danes had fled. The King was angry. He killed many people and burned down the homes of others. As a result of this there was a terrible famine. More than 100,000 Christian folk died of hunger.'

This was written by a monk who had trained in Normandy.

Sources 1 to 3 above give solutions to William's problems which you read about on page 3. On the table below match the problem to its best solution.

Problems	Solution
A	
B	
C	

Use an atlas to help you answer these questions.

1 Where is Poitiers? _____
2 What side do you think William of Poitiers supported? _____
3 Where is Worcester? _____
4 What side do you think Florence of Worcester supported? _____

William conquers England

Carefully read the three sources on page 4. They tell you how William took control of England. Then answer the questions below.

1. Underline the words below which you think best describe William.

kind	cruel	gentle	ruthless	greedy
generous	bloodthirsty		forgiving	good
royal	unfeeling	bad tempered		friendly

2. Explain why you underlined one of the words you chose in Question one. Mention the source that made you think William was like the word you underlined.

I underlined _____ because in Source _____ it said _____
_____
_____

3. Do you think William made a good start as King of England? Give a reason for your answer.
_____
_____
_____
_____

4. What were the results of William's treatment of the people around York?
_____
_____
_____
_____

5. Colour the map below showing the Norman conquest of England. Make each year a different colour.

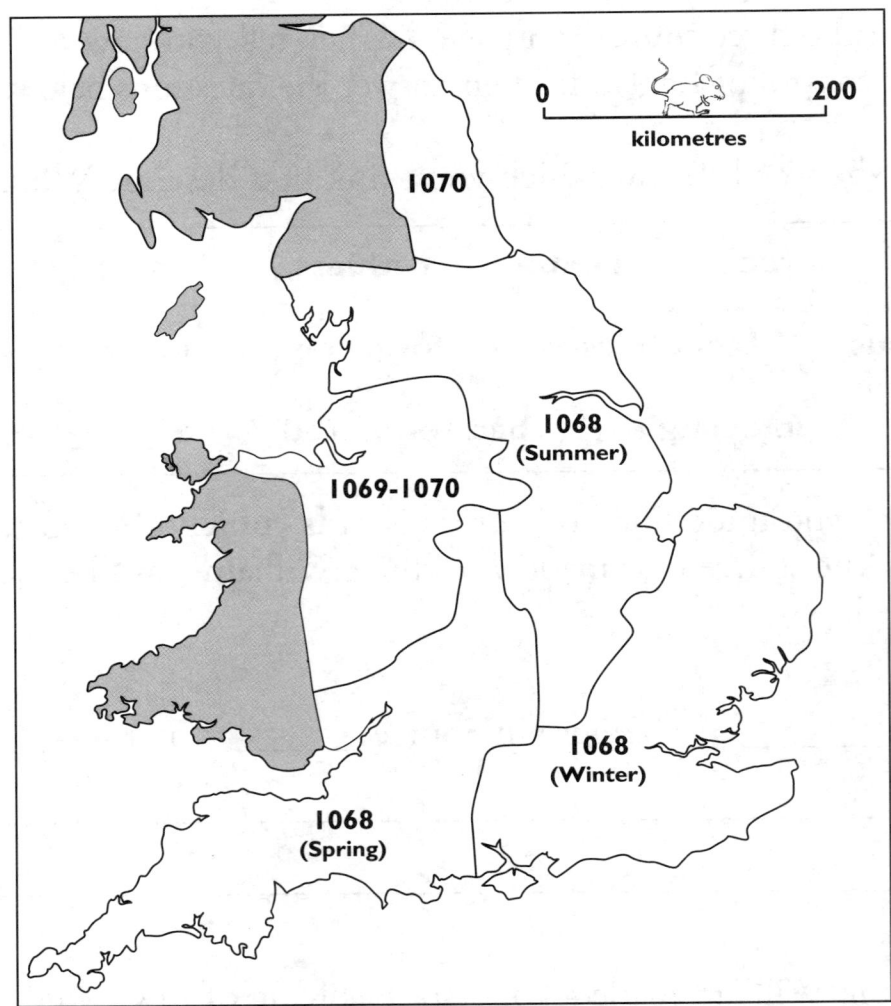

The Norman Conquest of England

6. In what year did William have most of England under his control? Write your answer as a full sentence.

_____
_____

7. Why do you think William wasted no time in getting control of all of England?

_____
_____
_____
_____

How did William keep control? 7

Although William was King of England not everyone wanted to obey him. Many English barons did not accept William as their king. William did not trust the barons because they might try to take the throne from him. The five things below could help William control England. Read them carefully and answer the questions on page 8.

A.
The Norman barons are your friends. Take the land off the English barons. Keep most of it yourself, but give some of it to your friends.

B.
If you make a big army everyone will be frightened of you. Make English people join your army so that they have to fight for you.

C.
Build lots of castles so that people can see how strong you are. Give them to your Norman friends.

D.
Ask everybody in the country how much money and things they own. Then make them pay taxes and use this money to pay for your army.

E.
You are the king. You can make the laws. If people break these laws, you can punish them or even fine them.

8 1. Why did William not trust the barons?

2. Write out the five things William could do to get control of England.

(i)

(ii)

(iii)

(iv)

(v)

3. Which two things do you think would be best to do? Explain why you choose them.

(a)

(b)

Motte and Bailey Castles

Read pages 20 and 21 of your textbook and answer the questions below.

1. Complete the passage below by filling in the missing words:

The Normans built castles to keep c_____ of the land they had captured and to p_____ themselves from the English. The earliest castles had to be built q_____ so they were put on the top of a mound of e_____ and made of w_____. These wooden castles were usually built by the people the N_____ had just c_____. These motte and b_____ castles were easy to attack as they could be b_____ by an enemy.

Missing words

wood	conquered	protect	Normans
earth	burnt	control	bailey	quickly

2. Why was a tower built on top of the motte?

_____

_____

_____

3. Give one reason why the English did not like the Norman motte and bailey castles.

_____

_____

_____

Label the castle

What type of castle is this? Write the name in the sentence beside the picture. Draw a line from each box to the correct place on the castle. Then write about each item in the box below its name.

The Keep	**Wooden bridge**

This is a _____ castle

The Moat	**The Motte**	**The Bailey**

Stone Castles

Using page 22 of your textbook label the areas marked 1 to 4 on the diagram of the keep castle below. Number 3 has been completed for you.

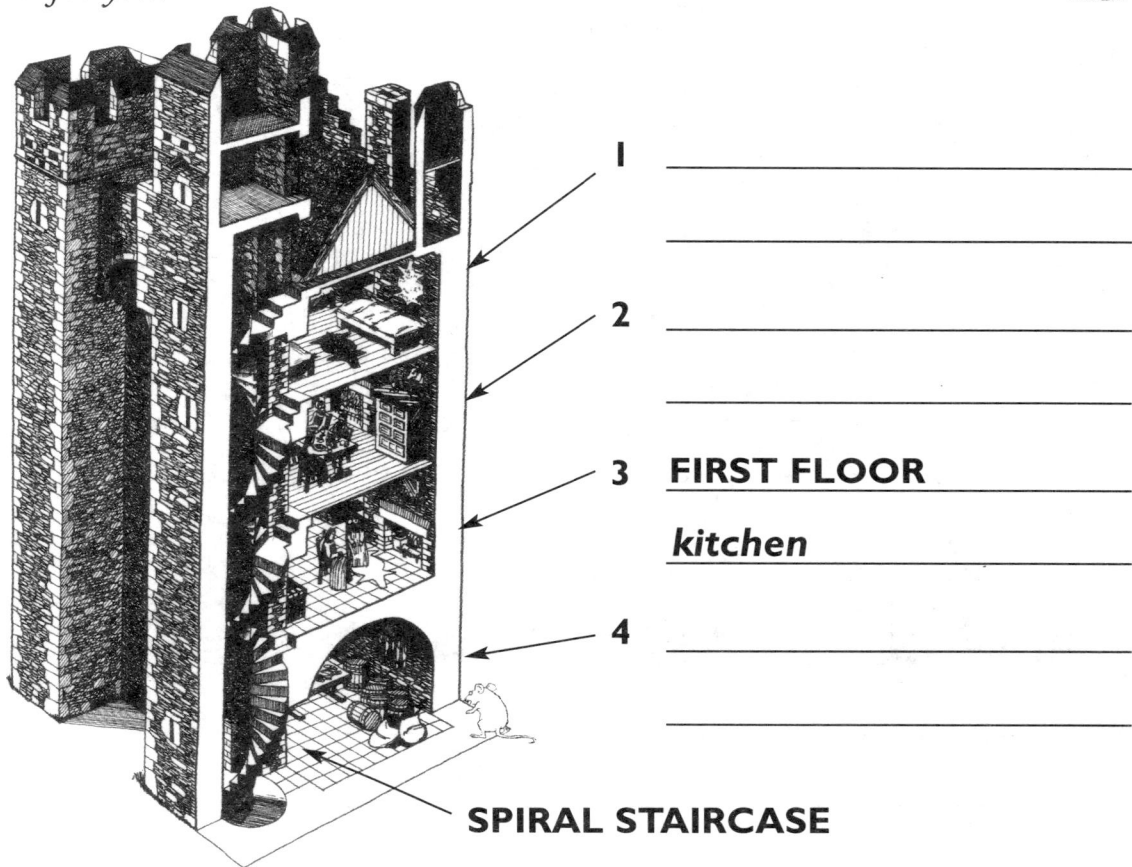

1 _____

2 _____

3 **FIRST FLOOR**
   kitchen

4 _____

SPIRAL STAIRCASE

1. Why did the keeps have spiral staircases?
_____
_____

2. How might the spiral staircases be useful if the castle was being attacked?
_____
_____

3. Most castles also had a well for water. Why do you think it was important to have a well?
_____
_____
_____

12 Defending a Castle

Read page 23 of your textbook.

1. Imagine you are defending the castle below. Name three things you would do to stop the enemy capturing the castle.

a. _____
_____

b. _____
_____

c. _____
_____

2. What was a siege?
_____
_____

3. Why did a siege not always work?
_____
_____
_____

Attack!

Read page 23 again.
You are the son or daughter of the man who owns this castle and you are inside it when it is being attacked. You keep a diary. Write an entry for your diary about the day shown in the picture. Your entry has been started for you.

When my servant woke me this morning

14 Planning a feast

Read pages 26 and 27 of your textbook.
Go to the library and find out more about the kind of food people ate in medieval times. Now write out your own menu for a feast in the Great Hall of the Lord of the Manor.

MENU

Now you have to tell everyone where to sit. Write the names of the guests in the places where you think they should sit.
You could photocopy these pictures, cut them out and stick them in the squares.

Lord of the Manor

Lord's youngest son **Lord's eldest son**

Lady of the Manor **Knight's wife**

Knight **Monk**

Top table

The Feudal System (1)

Read page 18 of your textbook and answer the questions below.

1. Match up the start of the sentences below with the proper endings.

STARTS

(a) The feudal system was how

(b) The feudal system was based on

(c) All the land in England

(d) The king gave land to the barons who

(e) The knights got land from the barons because

(f) The knights gave land to the peasants who

ENDINGS

(i) belonged to the king and the church.
(ii) they promised to fight for them.
(iii) had to work on their land and pay them taxes.
(iv) the Normans organised society in the Middle Ages.
(v) promised to be loyal and get knights to fight for him.
(v) who owned land.

16 The Feudal system (2)

Fill in the blank lines in the speech bubbles below.

The King

I own all the land but I cannot control it myself, so _____
_____
_____

Barons

We are loyal to the king and promise to _____
_____
_____

We give some land to our _____

Knights

We have been given land by the _____ and in return

we promise _____

We give some of our land to the _____

Peasants

We are very poor, but we have been given land by the _____

In return for this we must _____

The Domesday Survey

Read page 19 of your textbook and the passage below, then answer the questions which follow.

In 1085 William decided to find out exactly how much land he owned in England and what everyone else owned. He also wanted to find out what services every man had to do. He sent out clerks to every village in England to collect this information and it was written down in a large book called the **Domesday Book**. The Domesday Book was completed in 1086. You can see the Domesday Book in the Public Record Office in London.

1. Why did William have a survey of England carried out?
_____
_____

2. When was the survey carried out?
_____
_____

3. How was the survey carried out?
_____
_____
_____

4. Why do you think the king made the people swear an oath?
_____
_____

5. What is the name of the book in which the results of the survey is written?
_____

6. Where would you see this book today?
_____

7. How old is it now? _____

18 Country Life

Using pages 37 and 38 of your textbook complete the work given below.

1. Complete the passage below by filling in the missing words:

Most people in the Middle A_____ lived in a small v_____ of 20 to ____ families. The village was controlled by a l_____. Each villager had to

(i) work on the lord's l_____ several days a week;

(ii) use only fallen w_____ for fires;

(iii) m_____ the person the lord told them to.

The most important buildings in the village were the c_____, the manor house and the m_____.

MISSING WORDS

mill	wood	30	Ages	land
marry	lord	village	church	

2. Here is a plan of a medieval village. Colour the mill and the church in red.

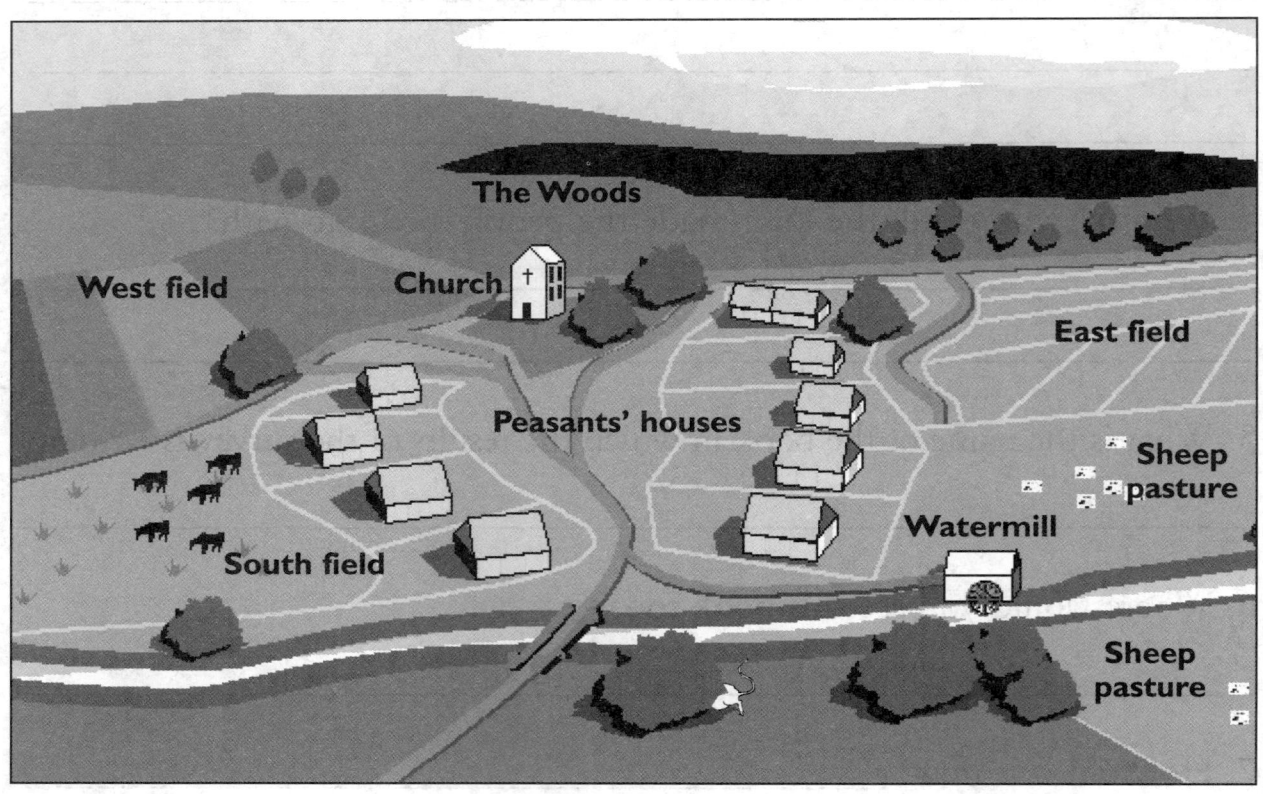

3. Match up the tops and tails. Draw arrows in your book to match them up.

TOPS	TAILS
1. People in the country had to get up early	(a) shops to go to such as we have today.
2. The farmer's cart was	(b) grow their own food and make their own clothes.
3. People in the Middle Ages didn't have	(c) to work all day in the fields.
4. Poor people had to	(d) pulled by oxen.

4. Look at the pictures on page 37 and 38. Name three types of work done by people in the country.

   a. _____

   b. _____

   c. _____

5. Do you think you or your family could grow your own food and make your own clothes? Explain your answer.

   _____
   _____
   _____
   _____
   _____
   _____

6. The pictures below show the kinds of things a peasant would be doing throughout the year. Imagine you are a peasant in the Middle Ages. Write a paragraph under each picture telling what work you do during each season of the year.

The Peasant's Year

Spring

Ploughing and sowing. Planting beans. Ditching.

Summer

Hay harvest. Weeding the corn, bird scaring, fencing.

Autumn

Corn harvest. Threshing. Killing and salting the animals.

Winter

Tree felling, clearing waste land, thatching and repair. Cutting holly and ivy for fodder.

Medieval Houses

Look at the plan of the peasant's house on page 34 of your textbook.

1. In the space below, draw your own plan of a peasant's house. Your drawing doesn't have to be nearly as complicated as the one in the book.

2. See if you can find out what wattle and daub is and what it was used for. Write what you have found out on the lines below.

_____
_____
_____
_____
_____
_____
_____

3. On the table below compare your house to the peasant's house.

	My House	Peasant's house
Number of Rooms		
Building Materials		
Windows		
Doors		
Roof		
Heating		
Furniture		
Beds		
Other		

4. Which house would you rather live in? Give reasons for your answer.

_____
_____
_____
_____
_____
_____

The Medieval Town

Read page 36 of your textbook.

Draw arrows between the tops and tails of the sentences below so that they read correctly. One has been done for you.

TOPS	TAILS
1. By 1300, there were	(a) sold their goods at markets.
2. People threw their rubbish	(b) were smaller than our houses today.
3. Houses in medieval times	(c) people had to put out their fires.
4. When the curfew bell sounded	(d) and there was always a danger from fire.
5. Many buildings were made of wood	(e) into the street.
6. Many craftsmen	(f) 7 million people in Britain.

2. Name one place where a town might grow up.

_____

3. Why were medieval towns smelly?

_____
_____
_____
_____

4. *Read this paragraph and then answer the questions below.*
Many traders were dishonest. Some of them had two sets of scales – one for buying and one for selling. Sometimes traders added dangerous ingredients, such as chalk dust instead of flour to bread. Anyone caught cheating was put in the stocks or pillory for a day. People could then throw mud or eggs at them, or even empty the chamber pot over them!

(a) Give two ways traders could cheat their customers.

_____

_____

(b) Why do you think they use different scales for buying and selling?

_____

_____

_____

(c) Here are pictures of the stocks and pillory.

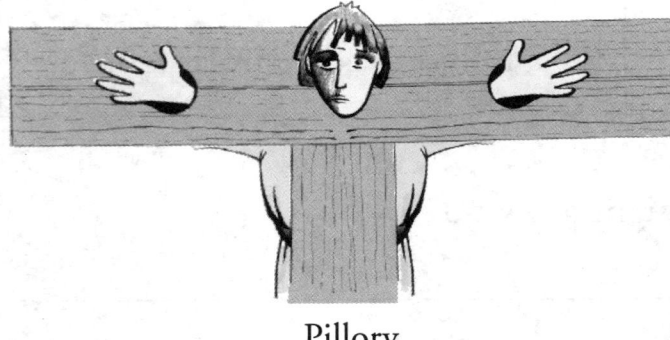

Pillory

Stocks

Do you think this punishment was fair? Give a reason for your answer.

_____

_____

_____

5. Look at this picture. You can see it in colour on page 36 of your textbook.

(a) What is the man in the picture doing? Answer in a full sentence.

_____

_____

(b) Do you think this man's trade was important in medieval times? Why do you think this?

_____

_____

_____

6. Often the sign over a shop told you what the shop owners did. Look at the pictures of two shop signs below. What do you think the owners of each shop did for a living?

This could be a sign for a _____ shop.

This could be a sign for a _____ shop.

7. Think of two more possible shop signs for medieval shops. Draw them and label them with the name of the shop.

This is a sign for a
_____ shop.

This is a sign for a
_____ shop.

8. Look at page 25 of your textbook and read the conversation between the two people on the right of the page. Write down possible surnames for the people they are talking about. For example, the first man would be talking about John Butcher.

_____
_____
_____
_____

9. Think of some surnames that have come from the jobs that people did in medieval times. Write down as many as you can and say what they did. For example, a draper would have sold clothes.

_____
_____
_____
_____

Norman clothes

Read pages 28 and 29 of your textbook. Now label the drawings below with the words in the box.

tunic	brooch	cloak		
long dress	girdle	shoes	wimple	

Compare Norman clothes with the clothes we wear nowadays.

Things that are the same:

_____

_____

Things that are different:

_____

_____

28 The Black Death 1348

Read pages 44 and 45 of your textbook, then answer the questions below in full sentences.

1. Where did the Black Death come from?
   _____

2. When did the Black Death arrive in Britain?
   _____

3. Describe how the Black Death affected people who caught it.
   _____
   _____
   _____

4. Draw a skull in the box below and then write on each line something people thought was either a cause or a cure of the Black Death.

Causes		**Cures**
_____		_____
_____		_____
_____		_____
_____		_____
_____		_____

This is one of the pictures from page 45 of your textbook, showing what people thought they could do about the Black Death. Complete the sentences below.

What people thought they could do about the Black Death.

1. Try not to breathe in toilet smells.
2. Houses where someone had the plague should be marked with a red cross.
3. Pray to God to stop his anger.
4. Build special pest houses outside the town.
5. Cover windows.
6. Carry sweet smelling herbs or flowers.
7. Do nothing and hope for the best.

5. If people thought the plague was caused by bad air, they _____

_____

_____

6. If people thought the plague was a punishment from God, they

_____

_____

7. If people thought the plague was spread by people, they _____

_____

_____

8. The Black Death was really caused by _____

_____

_____

9. Do you think rich people or poor people were more likely to catch the plague? Give reasons for your answer.

_____

_____

_____

_____

30 Key Words

Write the key words below beside their correct meanings.

feudal system	knight	pillory
Great Hall	motte	baron
bailey	moat	peasant
keep	siege	Black Death

1. A person with some land who worked for the Lord of the Manor _____

2. A person who held land from the king _____

3. A small hill for building a castle on _____

4. The plague of 1348 was known by this name _____

5. To surround a town or castle to attack it _____

6. The ditch going right round a castle _____

7. A method of holding land by giving service rather than money to the owner _____

8. A wooden frame with holes for the head and arms used to punish criminals _____

9. Outer courtyard in a motte and bailey castle _____

10. A castle's strong central tower _____

11. A heavily armoured soldier on horseback _____

12. The biggest room in a castle _____

A puzzle about the Normans in Britain

Answer questions 1 to 9 to check your answer to 1 Down is correct.

DOWN
1. The nickname of William of Normandy.

ACROSS
1. A building the Normans made for protection.
2. The people who ruled England before the Normans.
3. A Norman soldier on horseback.
4. To take a country by force.
5. A system to get land by giving service.
6. A person who worked the land for his lord.
7. A person who held land from the King.
8. A book that gives a record of England in 1086.
9. A wooden frame with holes for the head and hands where people were put for punishment.

32 What do you think of this workbook?

1. What did you think about the booklet? Was it helpful, boring, enjoyable, interesting, dull, easy, hard, fun, good or bad?

I thought the booklet was _____

_____

_____

_____

2. Which part of the booklet did you enjoy most? Explain why.

_____

_____

_____

3. Which part of the booklet did you least enjoy? Explain why.

_____

_____

_____

4. How would you improve the booklet?

_____

_____

_____

5. Do you think this workbook helped you learn about the Normans in Britain?

_____

_____

_____